Loyal Hearts, Happy Tails

Stories of Rescue, Devotion,
Heroism and Healing
for Those Who Love Dogs

Inspired
by Faith

Loyal Hearts, Happy Tails
©Product Concept Mfg., Inc.

Loyal Hearts, Happy Tails
ISBN 978-0-9886719-8-0
Published by Product Concept Mfg., Inc.
2175 N. Academy Circle #200, Colorado Springs, CO 80909

Written and Compiled by Patricia Mitchell, including guest authors
in association with Product Concept Mfg., Inc.

Loyal Hearts, Happy Tails

Animals are such agreeable friends—
they ask no questions; they pass no criticisms.
George Eliot

The love and devotion of dogs

is real and genuine, as anyone knows who has been blessed with a four-legged friend. Dogs stride by our side as we explore our corner of the world, and they're our faithful support when we're facing the challenges of life. Their lavish love is something we can depend on. The only reward they ask for is a pat on the head...and a biscuit is always welcome, too!

Loyal Hearts, Happy Tails is a collection of stories written by people who love dogs— people like you. These are stories that will bring back warm memories, prompt a few chuckles, draw a sympathetic tear, and perhaps make you wonder exactly who benefits most from canine love and affection! Each page of hope and healing, sweetness and courage, loyalty and companionship will surely touch your heart.

Dog tale after dog tale, you'll agree that happiness is life in the presence of a wonderful dog.

And Then Along Came Sweetpea

Mary Shields

My husband and I had just lost our black chow, Maxi. He was a bit of a rascal and a one-family dog, but we loved him dearly. After he passed away, we decided that we did not want to go through the pain of losing another pet, so we tore out the backyard fence and gave away all dog-related things. We cried for weeks, and to this day we still feel his presence.

Then one day we were on our daily walk, and ahead of us we noticed this sad-looking little dog, obviously lost. I approached her and knelt down to see if she had any collar or tags so I could call her owner, but she had nothing on her. While I was petting her, she gently laid her head on my knee. I said, "Oh, what a little sweetpea you are!"

She trotted after us and followed us home. I gave her some water and food and began to call everyone I knew who might want to take her in. She appeared to be part Sheltie, part shepherd as far as I could tell. She had beautiful silky hair and her eyes were full of gratitude and sweetness.

I notified the lost dog registry, posted flyers with her picture on it throughout the neighborhood, put an ad in the newspaper, and notified

Early on, when Dave had to go out of town, Willie would not leave the door of the house. Food and water had to be brought to him. Over time, the separation anxiety diminished, and Willie got comfortable being around other people. Dave had to give Willie a lot of love and patience in the meantime, but in return, Willie loved Dave unconditionally.

Sometime later Dave read a newspaper article about a dog in Turkey named Melek. She was a two-year-old English Setter mixed breed that had been hit by a car. A veterinarian came across the poor dog and took her to his clinic. He had to amputate her hind leg, but other than that, she was fine. He brought her to the shelter and a rescue group for her breed put out a worldwide alert that Melek needed a good home.

An American woman answered the call and made arrangements for Melek to come to the U.S. Once the woman got her, though, she realized that it wasn't a good match. Again, Melek found herself in an animal shelter. The local paper ran Melek's story and mentioned that interviews were being taken at the shelter for her adoption. She needed someone willing to give her a second chance at life.

Dave's not sure what made him decide that he and Willie needed her, but decide he did. Thinking there was no way he'd get another dog with special needs from the shelter, he tried not to get his hopes up, but after an initial interview, he was invited back for a second. This time he was asked to bring Willie. He had made it to the final few candidates! Some of the people at the shelter remembered Willie and could not believe how much better he was doing. Dave thinks that's what earned him the "yes" for Melek.

Today all three second-chancers are making good progress adjusting to each other and bonding as one happy, loving family.

WONDERFUL THINGS
CAN HAPPEN WHEN
WE'RE WILLING TO GIVE—
AND RECEIVE—
A SECOND CHANCE.

There is no difficulty that enough love
will not conquer;
no disease that enough love
will not heal;
no door that enough love
will not open;
no gulf that enough love
will not bridge;
no wall that enough love
will not throw down;
no sin that enough love
will not redeem...

Emmet Fox

Hurry Up, Bob!

Linda Alley

Bob was my valentine gift to my fiancé, Steve. Actually, a leash, dog bowls, and a coupon good for choosing a shelter puppy or dog of his choice was the gift. Steve was excited and had a name picked out before we got to the shelter— Bob.

The minute we saw the little black Lab mix, we knew we had found Bob. Once we got him home, Bob got a bath, food, and started almost immediately with his house training. As with all training, we needed a command. "I'm not going to tell a dog to 'go potty'," stated Steve. "We need to come up with something less babyish." After several suggestions, he decided on "hurry up, Bob."

My mind immediately flashed forward to the future, envisioning us running late, trying to wrangle kids, all kinds of paraphernalia, and Bob into a minivan. I could hear myself telling everyone to "hurry up" and Bob stopping dead in his tracks and urinating everywhere. I shared this vision with Steve, who brushed it off and assured me that would never happen. After I made a few more unsuccessful suggestions, it was decided to go with "hurry up, Bob" as the command. Steve was great at taking Bob out when necessary, including training him to go one last time before bed.

A week or so later, I was playing with Bob in our front yard when our next-door neighbor, a single woman, came over. She smiled as our sweet little pup ran over to her. "What did you name him again?" she asked.

"Bob," I replied.

She started—and then began laughing. Seeing the puzzled look on my face, she explained. "The other night I was getting ready for bed. I was back in the bedroom, and all of a sudden I heard a man's voice whispering, 'Hurry up, Bob!' Then I heard him say it again. I thought for sure there were two men outside, ready to break in! When I heard 'hurry up, Bob' yet again, I picked up the phone and was ready to dial 911. I paused, listening hard. But when I didn't hear anything more, I finally put the receiver down. But I didn't sleep a wink all night!"

I apologized profusely, we had a good laugh, and then Bob proceeded to "hurry up." Who knew that potty training a puppy could potentially end up involving the police?

It's the little things
    that tug on your heart.

Chasing Squirrels

C.E. Ross

There are few things in life that give you comfort like the love of a dog. Her name was Crimson, a 16 year old Visla who still played as if she was 5. Being a very experienced hunting dog, she passed her days in the backyard chasing squirrels and watching the birds in the trees. I'm sure she wished she could fly so her chase could have been more successful. Though she never actually caught a squirrel, her love of the chase was ever present.

Like so many nights when we would come home after work she would greet us with tail wags and wet kisses telling the whole family how close she was to having a successful hunt that day. After stories were told and love was shared it was time for dinner, another pastime that was always greeted with glee.

This night, however, would be like no other. As I was getting dinner ready, Crimson slipped on the kitchen floor, and grimaced in pain. That was the last time she could ever walk or so I thought. I immediately began to love her and tried to figure out exactly what had happened.

Knowing she was in pain, I moved her to her favorite spot on our couch and continued to shower her with affection. I knew this was serious, for at 16 she was very thin and frail like so many of our family friends who reach their older years.

The night progressed and it was clear she was not going to get up from her spot on the couch. Exhausted, I reluctantly went to bed. With thoughts in my head of all the good times we shared and tears in my eyes, I drifted off.

Early the next morning I felt something move next to me. To my surpise it was Crimson right by my side. As I opened my eyes she gently stretched out her paw and placed it on my chest. Once again, she was making sure that I was OK.

I still don't know how she was able to move from the couch and on to the bed but I do know that the love of a dog is timeless, precious, and one of a kind. A love that is truly unconditional.

Today I saw a squirrel, and my heart smiled.

Greyson

I will Always remember your great and loving personality. Your eyes bright green, Your face turned gray but, your personality didn't wear of. I cant wait to see you in heaven. For as long as I new you, you were a very behaved dog. I didn't Know you were going to pass 3 days after my birthday. It was a shoking suprise. The thing that you really loved was food. I love you so much.

(A message from my son)

20

A boy can learn
a lot from a dog:
obedience, loyalty, and the
importance of turning
around three times
before lying down.

Robert Benchley

Henry, the Ranch Dog

JoLynne Walz Martinez

When my husband and I were newly married, we regularly went to visit his parents at the ranch they operated in southern Missouri. They raised cattle, which my father-in-law worked on horseback with the assistance of his dog, Henry. When one of the cows or a calf got out of line, Henry would nip at its heels, returning it to the herd.

"Henry is one smart dog," my father-in-law would brag, "that when I'm working on some farm equipment and need a tool, all I have to do is tell Henry, 'I want a wrench', and he'll go get one for me."

My father-in-law was also proud of his 600 well-tended acres, which are so far out in the country that there is no light pollution from any city.

"I don't miss all the hard work," my husband told me when we were dating, "but you should see the night sky out there."

Work on the ranch is hard, and sometimes it can be dangerous. One summer when my husband was a teenager, a piece of equipment crushed his foot. Sometimes rattlesnakes threaten the cattle, so my father-in-law carries a big stick. And—although uncommon—there have been a few sightings of bears and mountain lions in the county.

On one of our visits when we were still newlyweds, after my husband's parents were asleep for the night, my husband appeared with a blanket and flashlight in hand.

"Let's go watch the stars." Taking his hand, I let him lead me through the fields where cattle were dreaming in the darkness.

A couple of fields away from the house, we crested a hill, where we spread our blanket. When my husband turned the flashlight off, my eyes took a moment to adjust…and there was the Milky Way spilling stars all over the sky above us.

Lying back on the blanket and holding hands, I felt like we were floating together above the sky in zero gravity, and, if we wanted, we could drift on forever through that gleaming sea of stars.

We lay there floating through the Milky Way for I don't know how long. And then I felt my husband's hand tense in mine.

Abruptly, he scrambled to his feet. Pulling me up by the hand, he gathered the blanket in his other arm and started striding off in the direction of the house.

"What is it?" I asked. "What's wrong?"

"Listen," he said.

I stopped for a moment but didn't know what he meant that I should listen for. Cicadas? Cows?

"Coyotes."

Yes, I heard them calling. "But I thought they never bothered people?" I said, sounding as puzzled as I felt.

"Pure coyotes don't," was my husband's response, "but around here there are packs of coyotes mixed with dogs. They're big, and they're not afraid of us." He tugged my hand again to pull me along. "At first I wasn't worried, because they were calling off in the distance," he said, "but then I realized they were getting closer. And now they're circling us."

I knew my husband well enough to know he wouldn't be afraid without good reason. We started walking as fast as we could in the darkness over uneven terrain. That flashlight didn't seem to cast near as much light on the way back from the hillside as it had on the way out.

And once I knew what to listen for, I realized my husband was right. The coyote-dog calls kept getting closer and closer, and they were coming from all sides.

We could have run, but that would have been an invitation to the pack to chase us. I am sure my pulse was racing much faster than my steps were! And then I felt it. A wet nose pressed into the palm of my free hand. I screamed.

Whirling around, brandishing the flashlight— the only weapon he had—my husband prepared to fight, and then we realized that it was no wild animal that had frightened me so.

It was Henry, the ranch dog.

All of the people of the house were asleep, but Henry was awake. Somehow he had realized we were in trouble, and he had come to herd us home.

Under Henry's protection, we arrived back safely. And you have never heard such grateful praise as that dog received! Not to mention more than one treat slipped into his food bowl.

My father-in-law is 82 now. He still works the ranch on horseback, but there are two new dogs helping keep those cows and calves in line. But my husband and I will always remember Henry. Like my father-in-law bragged, he was "one smart dog." And we tell anyone who will listen about how Henry, the ranch dog, rescued us on that starry night so many years ago.

The heavens declare the glory of God;
and the firmament sheweth his handywork.

Psalm 19:1

Just doin' my job.

Balto

A story of Endurance, Fidelity, and Intelligence

Who's that dog in Central Park? If you're looking at a sculpture of a sturdy Siberian Husky, meet Balto. Although his monument is in New York, he gained fame over three thousand miles away in Nome, Alaska.

In the winter of 1925, diphtheria broke out in Nome, hitting children and young people particularly hard. Antitoxin was available, but it was nearly a thousand miles away in Anchorage. The two planes that would have provided the fastest transport had frozen engines. Medics did the next best thing—they sent the serum by train as far as the tracks went, and then by relays of sled dog teams the rest of the way to Nome!

The dogs and their drivers carried their precious cargo through sub-zero temperatures and blinding blizzards. The effort was broadcast worldwide, and when the last team arrived in Nome, Balto was at the head of it. He instantly became the face of the rescue effort.

Inscribed on Balto's
plaque in Central Park
are these words:

DEDICATED TO THE INDOMITABLE SPIRIT
OF THE SLED DOGS THAT RELAYED ANTITOXIN
SIX HUNDRED MILES OVER ROUGH ICE,
ACROSS TREACHEROUS WATERS,
THROUGH ARCTIC BLIZZARDS FROM NENANA
TO THE RELIEF OF STRICKEN NOME
IN THE WINTER OF 1925.

ENDURANCE – FIDELITY – INTELLIGENCE

COURAGE IS RESISTANCE TO FEAR,
MASTERY OF FEAR,
NOT ABSENCE OF FEAR.

MARK TWAIN

Heaven Sent

Laurie Harper

Our home was a typical full and busy house that included a boy, a girl, two large dogs, a white rat, a husband who worked long hours, and me.

One night, as I tucked our 10-year old daughter, Megan, into bed, I noticed a shrine of pictures taped to her bedroom wall. As I looked closer, I could tell they were all pictures of Yorkshire Terrier dogs.

"Why all the pictures?" I asked.

"Because I'm praying every night for a Yorkie puppy," she replied with wide-eyed innocence.

"The last thing we need in this house is another dog!" I said with that tone of voice that mothers get when they hope to instill fear and trembling in the hearts of hearers.

As our custom, I closed my eyes and folded my hands in prayer with her. After our usual thanksgivings and blessings, she ended her prayer by saying, "And please, God, bring a Yorkie puppy to our house. I promise to love it and take good care of it." So she decided to bypass me completely and appeal to the Almighty!

I kissed her goodnight and went downstairs to finish a few things in the kitchen. Glancing out the window, I couldn't believe what I saw. A Yorkie puppy was sitting between our house and the neighbor's!

Without thinking, I yelled, "Megan! Come look what is outside in the neighbor's yard!" She came scampering downstairs, and of course she was certain that the puppy was an answer to her prayers!

The next day, we asked our neighbor, Donna, about the Yorkie. She told us that a friend of hers, Jill, had bought the dog, Kiya, after a recent divorce, but now had to work a second job. This meant Kiya had to spend most of her time alone in a kennel. Donna was dog-sitting Kiya for a few days while Jill decided what to do. We told Donna about Megan's shrine of pictures taped to her bedroom wall and her prayer for a Yorkie. Donna started to cry and told us that she had been praying for a better situation for Jill and for Kiya.

We decided as a family that we would offer to pay Jill for the privilege of taking Kiya.

When the time came for us to meet Jill and make her the offer, Megan and I were so nervous that we felt like we were going to a child's adoption interview. We assured Jill that we would love and take very good care of Kiya. She would have a fenced backyard to run and play in with our other dogs. We agreed on a price and after a tearful last hug, Jill placed Kiya in Megan's arms.

Kiya adjusted very quickly to her new home and our other dogs. The only thing that took her some time to get used to was that of a male voice. She had only lived with females until she moved in with us. Every time the men in the house spoke, she put her ears back and ran out of the room, looking quite offended. Megan and I thought she was one smart dog!

Megan held true to her promise to us and to God, and loved and cared very well for her. To this day, we think of our sweet Kiya as the dog that was heaven sent.

NOTHING IS TOO SMALL
A SUBJECT FOR PRAYER,
BECAUSE NOTHING IS TOO
SMALL TO BE THE SUBJECT
OF GOD'S CARE.

HENRY THOMAS HAMBLIN

I love this little house because
It offers after dark,
A pause for rest, a rest for paws,
A place to moor my bark.

Arthur Guiterman

The Pup with His Head in a Can

Patricia Mitchell

When Janice, a teacher, and her young son John were driving to school one morning, she noticed a small black animal thrashing around in the weeds near the road. Being a cat-lover and thinking there was a kitten in distress, Janice pulled over, stopped the car, and stepped into the weeds to retrieve the animal.

As she approached, she realized what had happened—the creature had its head stuck in a food can! Quickly she scooped up the animal, which turned out to be not a kitten, but a puppy. She couldn't remove the can without the jagged edges injuring him, so she handed the writhing bundle to her son, and she drove to the first convenience mart she saw.

The clerk at the convenience mart used a pry to get the can safely off the pup's head, freeing the trembling animal. Though John begged his mom to let him keep the puppy, she said no—they already had a temperamental Siamese cat in the family, and she didn't want the care of a dog. Instead, she said, they would get food and water for him, take him to school, and see if someone there could adopt him.

Ask a group of K-8 students if anyone would like a puppy, and watch dozens of eager hands shoot into the air! But phone calls to parents just as quickly quashed young hopes and the pup's chance of a home with one of the students.

After a day of stroking, cuddling, feeding, and nuzzling, the pup still had no place to go. Whimpering softly in the now-silent classroom, he watched as Janice loaded her lesson plans and take-home papers into her tote bag. She met John's pleading eyes as he waited by the door. "Okay," she said, "we'll take him, and if Dad agrees, we'll keep him."

John named the pup Blackie. When Blackie first entered the house, he and the Siamese came to an immediate understanding. With a hiss and a few flicks of her claws across his nose, she taught him the rules: no playing, nudging, or sniffing unless specifically invited by Me, the Queen of the House. With that, she curled up and went to sleep. Blackie abided by the rules, siding with John, who was also disdained by the Siamese cat. Together they formed a team—and became the best of best friends.

Blackie proved himself the perfect family dog. He possessed a natural friendliness that won the hearts of Mom, Dad, and everyone in the neighborhood. He was John's fishing buddy, hiking companion, and backyard playmate.

He lived with Mom and Dad while John attended college, and then joined John when he had his own place. No visit back home that John made, however, would be complete without the back door of his car opening and a happy-go-lucky black dog lopping out!

In later years, his muzzle speckled with white, Blackie slowed down and gradually his health declined. When he was gone, Janice felt his loss deeply.

"For a dog that started out with a can on his head, he did all right," she said, holding Queen of the House on her lap, "but there will never be another dog I could love as much as I loved Blackie." The Queen yawned, stretched, and took a nap, her authority intact. He was, after all, only a dog.

A dog is the only thing
on earth that loves you
more than he loves himself..

Josh Billings

Who's the Newbie?

Who's this critter that invaded my domain?

I used to be the one they ooohed and aaahhed over, the one they coddled and cooed to. But then one day they came home with another little wiggly being, this one wrapped in a flannel quilt. Boy, did they ever make a fuss over him! They still do.

At first I didn't think much of him—all he did was eat and sleep, eat and sleep. Well, that wasn't such a bad plan, I figured, and at least he had his own bed. Then I took to snoozing right next to his bed, you know. He was such an itty bitty creature, and something told me that I should watch out for him.

Lately he's started doing a few more things, and sometimes my people put us together on a blanket to play. He likes to push his rubber ball toward me, and then he giggles like crazy when I gently nudge it with my nose back to him. Some humans amuse easily, don't they?

He sits in a high chair and gets his own plate of food now, too. He sure isn't any good at finding his mouth! He clutches his spoon, digs into his cereal, and then takes a wild swing in the general direction of his face. Most of the time he flips the food on the floor. What's not to like about that? I get to lick up a yummy dessert every day just by showing up at his dinner time!

And another thing. Before he didn't seem to know I existed, but now he reaches out to feel my fur and pat my head. I like that. Sometimes he grabs my tail, and my humans say, "No, no!" But that's not a problem, because I can see that his heart is in the right place.

Things just might work out between us after all.

The happiness of life is made up of minute fractions—the little, soon-forgotten charities of a kiss or smile, a kind look, a heart-felt compliment, and the countless infinitesimals of pleasurable and genial feeling.

Samuel Taylor Coleridge

A Little Help from My Friend

Mary Shields

Maxi was our 50-pound black chow. Though he looked like a cuddly black bear that you would just want to put your arms around and hug, this would not have been a good idea. Maxi loved my husband and me, but everyone else was suspect. At night, he'd patrol the house to make sure there were no intruders and during the day, he kept watch in the yard.

Our other dog was Puffy. She was a 7-pound toy poodle who loved everyone, including Maxi. Fortunately, Maxi loved her back. They'd sit in a chair by the front window together, Maxi on the seat and Puffy on the back of the chair. They would watch out the window for us to come home at the end of the day, and also bark the squirrels off the lawn. They both were allowed out in the yard without leashes, as they stayed in our yard—well, most of the time, anyway.

One day they were outside and a sizable dog wandered into our yard. For Maxi this was not allowable! The two of them got into a tussle, and clearly Maxi was losing the battle. Brave little Puffy to the rescue!

First she started to bark, but that didn't do anything to deter the stray. So then she went after the stray's hind legs, nipping and biting for all she was worth. This was just enough to distract the stray, and Maxi was able to get the upper hand (or paw, as would be the case) and chase the dog out of our yard. Puffy was so proud that she was able to help her big brother!

Well, the story continues. The next day, the owner of the stray dog was driving past our house with her dog in the car.

Maxi realized that the dog in the car was the same one that he and Puffy had run into earlier that day. Maxi chased after the car and planted himself in front of it, causing the lady to stop the car. Her dog leaped out the window, and he and Maxi had another go-round!

This time Maxi was in charge and the other dog sensed that this was not going to end well. He turned tail and jumped back into the car through the window, leaping over the hapless driver. The lady was so distraught that she sped off.

After that day, Maxi resumed being Puffy's protector, but he always welcomed her help when enemies threatened their turf!

Don't judge a dog by his size.
It's the size of his heart that matters.

We take care of our health,
we lay up money,
we make our roof tight
and our clothing sufficient,
but who provides wisely
that he shall not be wanting
in the best property of all—friends?

Ralph Waldo Emerson

Annie

A Story of Good Cheer and Hospitality

During a stop at a rural depot, a trainman spotted a thin, mangy, pregnant mutt roaming in search of a meal. Even though these were hard times, when many people had barely enough to feed themselves and their family, the trainman picked up the dog and brought her aboard. That's how she ended up at the train station in Fort Collins, Colorado, which, despite a no-dogs policy, became her new home.

Annie quickly made friends with railroad workers and travelers alike. When passengers alighted, she'd nuzzle willing hands held out to her, even, as the story goes, licking the tears from the faces of soldiers returning from the battlefields of World War II. Her fame grew, and soon everyone who alighted at Fort Collins was trying to get Annie's attention—sometimes even before greeting their own families!

Upon her death, the train crew buried their beloved Annie in the rail yard, now a tiny pet cemetery and historical landmark at the Downtown Transit Center in Fort Collins. Her headstone bears the inscription:

*Inscription at the base
of Annie's statue
in Fort Collins, Colorado*

FROM THE C&S MEN TO ANNIE OUR DOG,
1934-1946.
ADOPTED BY RAILROAD WORKERS IN 1934,
ANNIE SPENT HER LIFE AS THE UNOFFICIAL
AMBASSADOR TO FORT COLLINS, GREETING
PASSENGERS AT THE TRAIN DEPOT UNTIL 1948.
HER LEGEND SERVES AS AN INSPIRATION
TO ALL WHO READ IT.

Miss Daisy

Laurie Harper

Joyce and her husband, Carl, had just lost
their beloved dog to old age, and decided their
home needed another canine presence. They
wanted to help a dog that needed a family, so
they went to the local animal shelter. In one of
the cages was a beautiful yellow Lab mix; she
was pregnant. The shelter's director said that
she had been picked up as a stray. Though the
director felt there would be little problem finding
homes for her pups, Mom would be a different
story. That's all Joyce and Carl needed to hear!
They agreed to come back for her after she gave
birth and the pups were old enough to be on
their own.

After her pups were born, the people at the
shelter took a picture of Mom surrounded by
all her newborns to give to Carl and Joyce. The
couple named her Daisy, and Daisy fit into her
new family with ease. Carl and Joyce never
regretted their decision. They proudly displayed
the framed photo of Daisy with her newborn
pups right alongside their other family photos.

As the years passed, Joyce's health started to
deteriorate, and she was forced to give up doing
a lot of her usual outdoor activities. She had to

spend most of her time in the house, and Daisy became her constant companion. It was as if she understood Joyce's health issues were serious and her days were numbered.

I arrived at their house one afternoon to take Daisy to my house for a few days while Carl and Joyce went out of town. Joyce was giving me all of Daisy's supplies, and as we were saying our good-byes, I leaned toward Joyce to give her a hug. Suddenly, Daisy jumped toward me and forced herself between Joyce and me. I had to fight back the tears as I witnessed such true devotion and love. Joyce just laughed and patted Daisy on the head and told her it was okay. We hugged.

We lost Joyce a few months after that day. Whenever I visit their home and see Daisy with Carl, I know that he has a true and devoted friend for life.

Friendship is a sheltering tree.
Samuel Taylor Coleridge

Sailor and Me

by Buck, with a little help from Sue Englert

They got me a sister. I don't remember asking for a sister. In fact, I kind of liked being the only dog in the house, getting all of the attention—all of the time! It had been that way for about five years, and it was fine with me.

I remember when they first brought me home. I was the last pup left out of all of my brothers and sisters. I didn't know where they all went, and I wondered why I wasn't going anywhere, until the day I met the big guy. I knew right away that he and I were going to get along just fine because he let me sit in the front seat and he petted me all the way home. When we got there, I met the tall girl, and she was really excited to see me.

We got back in the car and they took me to the place where I first met the short lady. She was in a room with a bunch of kids, and they all wanted to pet me until a bell rang—then all the kids were all in a hurry to leave, except one.

He was a blond boy who paid special attention to me, and I knew that he and I would be best friends forever. After all, he had the same color fur as I did!

After a few minutes, the big guy, the short lady, the tall girl, and the blond boy and I all piled into the car and went home together. Life was good! They called me Buck, so I started answering to it. They took me outside a lot and set me down in the grass while they just stood there. I couldn't figure out what they were doing that for, but they did it every time I went to the bathroom inside the house.

One time, the big guy took me out and set me down on the grass even though I hadn't even gone to the bathroom in the house. I realized I actually had to go, so I did it on the grass. He got really excited, so I decided right then to go to the bathroom on the grass instead of in the house every time just to make him happy. It's weird how happy that made him and the short lady!

When it got dark, they would all go up some stairs, but I had to stay downstairs and sleep in a metal crate. I didn't like that because I wanted to be with my people, so I decided I was going to figure out how to go up those stairs, too. I tried and tried, and one day, I just went right up! After that, I followed them every time they went up there.

The rooms up there were different. They had beds in them, and I didn't think I would ever be tall enough to get up on one of those! It was OK, though, because the blond boy would pick me up and put me on the bed with him. I decided that was a much better place to sleep than that cold metal crate! He seemed to like having me there, too.

Eventually, the big guy put the crate out in the garage, and it stayed there. That made me really happy.

The tall girl was in college when I met her, so she didn't live with us at the house all of the time. But the blond boy was still in high school, so he was around a lot, and I liked that.

We wrestled and ran, and I chased him and he chased me. He kicked a ball and I ran after it. He threw a ring and I brought it back to him.

Those were the good old days…then the blond boy went off to college. All of a sudden, it was just me and the big guy and the short lady most of the time. It was lonely at first, but then after we all got used to it, it was actually kind of nice. I learned to sleep on the blond boy's bed by myself, or sometimes I would sleep on the floor next to the big guy. He and the short lady and I would go for walks and sit on the couch and watch TV and hang out in the back yard.

Then one day, everything changed again.

They brought her home—my little sister. I was perfectly fine without her. She was scared of me at first, and she knew nothing—nothing at all! I had to teach her everything, because she would just sit in the middle of the room and whimper.

She wasn't even little like me when I first came here. I immediately sniffed every corner of the house, up and down. But she couldn't, because she didn't even know how to go up and down stairs! She would just stand at the bottom of the stairway and cry.

I showed her how to go up, but she still just stood there and cried. I showed her how to go down, but she still stood there. I went up and down and up and down, and finally one time, she followed me up! I was so glad because that crying was really getting on my nerves. I won't even mention what I had to go through to teach her to go back down!

When my people introduce us to other people, they say, "The yellow one is Buck and the black one is Sailor. She's a rescue." I'm not sure what that means, exactly, but Sailor's weird about some things.

One thing is, she doesn't like toys. What kind of dog doesn't like toys? She won't even chase a ball when they throw it! (Some retriever she turned out to be!) And when I get the tug rope, she just looks at me like, "Go ahead. Take the rope. I don't care." But when I run, she runs beside me and tries to bite my ears. I can't figure out why, but it sure is annoying!

Overall, though, I guess it's really not so bad having her around. When the people are gone, we're here together. When it storms, I'm not the only scaredy dog in the house. It's more fun to go for walks with two of us instead of just me. And when I get in trouble, she gets in trouble too, because the people can't figure out which one of us did whatever we're getting in trouble for. That's kind of funny.

The tall girl got married and she has her own dog now. With the blond boy in college and not here very much, the big guy and the short lady seem to like having Sailor and me around.

I didn't ask for a little sister, but the short lady and the big guy always tell me what a good big brother I am, and then they pet me behind my ears. I guess it's OK. Sailor can stay.

The Good, the Bad, and the Ugly

Laurie Harper

Whoever came up with "the good, the bad, and the ugly" must have shared their home with a Labrador. Over the 36 years that my husband and I have been married, we have shared our home with three Labs, so we know. All three lived over ten years, and each has left us with many good, some bad, and a few ugly memories—all of them, in hindsight, apt to bring warmth to our hearts and smiles to our faces.

Let's start with the good. A Lab:

- Deals gently with children. Our son once decided to bite our Lab's nose (don't ask me why). He didn't pay him back in kind—not even a nip!
- Chases rabbits out of the garden. I love to plant flowers in my garden and the rabbits love everything I plant. As a rabbit sat nibbling on my hostas, I was never so proud of my yellow Lab when he chased it right into the neighbor's yard! (Let it feast on their hostas for a change!)
- Gives new meaning to the word loyal. As I lay in bed recuperating from surgery, I had a furry companion at my side to snuggle with and keep me warm.

But there's the bad. A Lab:

- Jumps onto furniture with muddy paws. We bought a brand new beige sofa and the day it was delivered, it was raining. The delivery truck was barely out of sight when we turned to see our wet, muddy Lab rolling all over it.
- Eats dessert first. I took a cake out of the oven and went for a walk while it cooled. When I returned home, there was no sign of the cake or the cake pan on the counter. But I did find a sleeping Lab, the cake completely gone and the pan licked clean! So much for our dessert that night.
- Adds unwanted color to carpets. Once I returned home to find that my young daughter had gotten into my lipstick and shared it with our Lab. He had decorated the carpet with Very Berry Red lipstick! I was so relieved that it wasn't what I first thought—blood—that I couldn't be mad at either of them.

And there's the ugly. A Lab:

- Believes wood, plastic, and leather are essential parts of their food pyramid. My antique dresser knobs are now little nuggets of wood. Sigh.
- Does not see a difference between leather and cloth. Our leather sofa has long scratches on it because our Lab tried to fluff up the leather before taking his afternoon nap. Another sigh.
- Laps stagnant water whenever discovered. We had a creek that ran next to the park and our Lab found it a great place to get a drink from and take a quick dip in before we returned home. Eeeeew!

Yes, having a Lab can be bad and maybe even a little ugly at times, but somehow the loyalty, gentleness, playfulness, companionship, and overall lovability make it all worthwhile!

You're my best friend and companion,
the one I can always trust
and though our language is not of words,
it's understood by us.
If there's one thing in life to aim for
I can only hope to be
the good and admirable person
you seem to see in me.

What's in a Number?

Reflections of a Senior Soul

They say you can't teach an old dog new tricks. Well, that's not true, at least not with me. Though I'm not quite as quick on my paws as I used to be—but who is?—I think I'm up to learning a new trick or two. But what I really need right now is a new home.

We senior citizens here at the shelter—and there are several of us—have lost our old families for a number of reasons. But we're a forgiving and understanding sort. We've lived long enough to know that some things happen in people's lives that make it impossible for them to continue taking care of us. After all, we're not naive pups anymore...yet that's why a lot of people who walk up and down the aisles here pass us by!

Sure, unlike most puppies, we might need to take our meds, so that's something we'll have to talk about. But I can tell you this for sure: When you bring one of us home, here's what you'll get:

- A smart, socialized dog. We seniors know how to live with a family, because we used to have one. You won't have to teach us much in that department! Just show us around and be patient with us while we learn how we can please you, and then we're good to go—no long puppy training sessions needed!
- A calm, settled dog. We've got some spunk left, but most of us won't be jumping all over you, your guests, your furniture, and who knows what else! No rambunctious puppies among us—we outgrew that a long time ago!
- A devoted dog. Yes, we've got a few years under our pelts, but we've got a lot of love left to give. And isn't that what it's all about?

Please, won't you stop for a minute and greet me on your next trip past my kennel? There's no trick at all to loving a not-so-old dog like me!

HOME IS WHERE THE HEART IS.

PROVERB

'Tis sweet to hear the
watch dog's honest bark
Bay deep-mouthed welcome
as we draw near home;
'Tis sweet to know there
is an eye will mark
Our coming and look
brighter when we come.

George Gordon, Lord Byron

A Place in the Heart

Laurie Harper

If you have ever owned a dog, then you have been blessed by:

- Comfort
- Ability to make you smile after a long day
- Gentle licking
- Eagerness to please
- Unending loyalty
- Playfulness
- Tolerance

Ask anyone about their dog, and you're likely to see a slow smile cross their face. Then they'll tell you a dog story. It might be something funny, or sad, heartwarming, silly, heroic, but they will have a story. Ask the name of their first dog, and they can tell you in an instant, followed by a heart-warming story. Some dog owners incorporate the dog's name for a computer password, or choose it as a security question.

It seems God knew there would come a day when some of us would need a non-judgmental companion to be a part of our lives...someone to help us carry our burdens, loves us without judgement, and showers us with heartwarming memories forever. Maybe that's why He created dogs.

How can we say thank you to our furry best friend? We say it with a ride in the car, a walk in the park, and a great big space in our hearts.

Gratitude is the heart's memory.
Proverb

Greyfriars Bobby

A Story of Love and Loyalty

Bobby, a Skye terrier in nineteenth-century Edinburgh, Scotland, remains to this day a symbol of canine devotion and companionship.

According to tradition, John Gray, a constable with the city police department, adopted the long-haired dog to work with him on night watch. Gray named him Bobby, appropriate for an official police dog. Apparently Bobby served well, both as another set of eyes and ears (not to mention a sharp nose!) through the dark streets of Edinburgh, but as Gray's faithful companion.

When his master died, Bobby trotted along with the funeral procession to the cemetery—wouldn't leave. Though the cemetery keeper drove him out many times, Bobby kept coming back until the keeper finally relented. Well-wishers fed and protected Bobby for 14 years until he died. Though it wasn't common practice to bury animals in the cemetery, Bobby was laid to rest not far from Gray.

The following year, a local patron commissioned a statue of Bobby, which stands at the southern end of the George IV Bridge in Edinburgh. You will find a plaque with this inscription:

A TRIBUTE TO THE AFFECTIONATE FIDELITY OF GREYFRIARS BOBBY. IN 1858 THIS FAITHFUL DOG FOLLOWED THE REMAINS OF HIS MASTER TO GREYFRIARS CHURCHYARD AND LINGERED NEAR THE SPOT UNTIL HIS DEATH IN 1872 WITH PERMISSION, ERECTED BY BARONESS BURDETT-COUTTS.

~ Inscription on Bobby's granite headstone
Greyfriars Churchyard

To this day, visitors to Bobby's gravesite and his statue find flowers and dog toys left by Bobby's many friends and fans!

Let his loyalty and devotion be a lesson to us all.

The Right Family

Dorie Allington

How do you know when a tiny, terrified dog has found the right family?

Our home felt empty after the loss of our beloved dog Paisley, and that's when we felt led to become fosters for an animal rescue organization.

Butterfly was a little white mixed-breed Papillon that came to us in very bad shape. Whenever someone would come near her, she'd run away, cower in a corner, and leave a puddle behind out of fright. No one could pick her up. She didn't know anything about stairs, couches, or chairs. She had no idea that she was supposed to do her business outside, or that it was okay—and a lot of fun!—to roll around in a pile of leaves.

Finally, after weeks of special care and gentle coaxing, she was ready for us to find her a forever family.

After the word went out that she was available, I got a call from a couple that had seen her picture online and wanted to meet her that day, even though they lived in a rural area several hours' drive away. I said that they were welcome to come over and that I would wait for them.

When the couple arrived, I was surprised. If it's true that people look like their dogs, certainly this couple didn't look like little Butterfly! While Butterfly was a frail six-pound slip of a girl, the man standing in front of me was a massive, burly man with tattoos up and down his arm and across his neck. I'd tend to match him up with a Labrador or Mastiff!

His petite wife, I thought, might be the one who's interested in a Papillon. Smiling at my own imaginings, I invited the couple in.

Holding Butterfly in my lap, I spoke to them at length about her painful background and her ongoing medical needs. It's vitally important that people understand the extent of care a formerly abused dog often requires. They weren't put off by anything I told them. Then I stood up, handed Butterfly to the woman, and left the room so the couple could get to know Butterfly and talk about what they wanted to do.

In about ten minutes, the woman called me in. ""We want to give her a home," she said. And that's when I saw dainty little Butterfly contentedly nestled in the big man's brawny tattooed arms. When I looked up at the man, I was overwhelmed to see that tears were streaming down his face. "No one will ever hurt her again," he said, "I promise."

I had no doubt in my mind that he was telling the truth.

After a while, I said the prayer I always do following those tearful yet joyful good-byes: "Thank you, God, for guiding us to the right family for this little dog."

IF I CAN STOP ONE HEART
FROM BREAKING,
    I SHALL NOT LIVE IN VAIN.
EMILY DICKINSON

A Good Dog's Prayer

Patricia Mitchell

Yippee, God! They picked me out!
Chose me from all the rest!
Was it my coat or size or eyes
That made them like me best?

I sure don't know, but certainly glad
This family took me home,
'Cause now I have a bed and yard
To call my very own.

They say I'm smart, and that's the truth!
I learn commands with ease.
I watch my manners in the house,
And always hope to please.

They take me out for morning walks,
I guard the house each day,
Until I hear a car drive in—
And then it's time to play!

When I do tricks that make them laugh,
They give me tasty treats.
When I come in on rainy days,
They wipe my muddy feets.

My doggie life is good, dear God,
And good for people, too.
You've blessed us with each other's love—
My heart gives thanks to You.
Amen

A Letter To My Foster Mom

Dear Foster Mom,

It's been awhile since we said good-bye but I know you haven't forgotten me. And I want you to know I haven't forgotten you, either.

The world has changed so much for me it's hard to believe. For so long, I was in that bad place in a tiny cage where day after day, turning into year after year, nothing changed and no one cared about me. I don't like to think about that. I like to remember the day some humans came and took me—and many others like me—away from that place.

I did not trust humans. Humans had not been kind. But then came you. I don't know what you saw in me, but something made you able to see past my dirty, matted fur…my sore body and my limp…and the fear I had of everything, even you. Something in your heart made you want to give me a chance.

When you took me home I had no idea what was going to happen to me. Everything was scary. I just wanted to hide under a desk and hope no one would see me. The other people in the house would try to reach out to me and touch me but I just moved further back. I did not know if the human hands would grab me and make me hurt.

Then there was the world outside to learn about! There was sun and sky, rain and clouds. There was also grass. It was strange and I didn't feel sure about that at all.

One very hard thing to understand was about when I needed to...you know. When I did that thing in the house your mouth went down and your eyes were like a cloud. When I did that outside, your mouth went up and your eyes had sunshine. You were very patient because it took me a big while to understand.

We were together a long time and I could feel a big change in my heart. We visited a human and her short boy human. They were gentle like you and their mouths went up. Later, we visited again, but this time, you held me lots and then gave me to the boy human. You were walking out the door and telling me this was my forever home. Your mouth went up but your eyes had rain. I was confused but I had learned to trust you and something told me it was all right.

And it was all right, Foster Mom. I have a home and love and all I could wish for. Thank you for seeing something in me and loving me through my tough change. Thank you for giving me a chance. I will never forget you.

COMPASSION BRINGS LOVE,
LOVE BRINGS HOPE,
HOPE BRINGS JOY.

Rudy, The Museum Dog

Laurie Harper

He gets up bright and early, has a quick breakfast and heads off to the boat museum in Minnesota for a full day's work. He greets guests, helps with tours, and even licks a few envelopes for a membership mailing.

No, I'm not talking about the museum director, Bruce. I'm talking about Bruce's yellow Lab whose name is Rudy. Last year, by a unanimous vote, Rudy was designated the boat museum's mascot after coming to work with Bruce a few days a week. Now, by popular demand, he's at his post almost every day that the museum is open.

Rudy has even earned his own section in the museum's newsletter. In *The Wag from Rudy*, he shares his dog's-eye view of museum happenings. In a recent column, for example, Rudy thanked the volunteers for their pats and attention, and another special volunteer for her endless supply of treats.

In addition to his duties around the building, Rudy guards the museum gardens. He makes sure those very dangerous geese don't come waddling in as if they owned the place. He takes great pride in chasing the trespassers right off the museum property.

It's rumored around the museum that Rudy hopes to get promoted soon. He'd like to be made captain, because he sure loves boats—and boat rides!

THE GRAND ESSENTIALS
TO HAPPINESS IN THIS LIFE
ARE SOMETHING TO DO,
SOMETHING TO LOVE,
AND SOMETHING TO HOPE FOR.
JOSEPH ADDISON

Love at First Sight

Patricia Mitchell

He saw her for the first time one Saturday morning at the dog park. While his feisty little Pomeranian, Ginger, frolicked with the park's small-sized regulars, Samuel furtively checked out a girl he had never seen before. Appearing as disinterested as possible, he noted her long, flowing hair, healthy complexion, and confident walk. She was accompanied by a tall, sleek Doberman. He noticed that as she let her dog off-leash, the dog ran in graceful circles around the girl, never straying far from where she stood.

Meanwhile, Ginger had darted off to the far side of the park with a bunch of spirited miniatures and a couple of pups that someone had brought over. "I must look pretty wimpy," he muttered to himself. "She's got this macho dog and I've got this frou-frou lapdog."

His manliness at stake, Samuel vowed to remedy the situation. Whistling for Ginger, who ignored him completely, he made up his mind to adopt a large, substantial dog. He hoped the girl wasn't looking as he struggled to extract Ginger from her playgroup wrestling together at the edge of the pond.

Visiting the animal shelter that afternoon, Samuel met just the dog he was looking for—a Great Dane mix named Max. Though Max was an older dog, he was still active and energetic. Samuel liked Max's sturdy physique, poised demeanor, and intelligent eyes. He introduced Max to Ginger, and the two dogs hit it off immediately.

On the following Saturday, Samuel approached the dog park with newfound confidence. While Ginger trotted excitedly, pulling at the leash, the stately, mature Max walked obediently alongside his master. Ginger, as was her habit, zigzagged from one spot to the next, Max kept pace with Samuel.

Ginger's uncontrolled exuberance reminded Samuel of his baby sister, Trina. She always wanted to tag along with him and his buddy,

Jeff. He and Jeff, with heads held high, preferred to ignore the nuisance kid scurrying to keep up with their long strides and yelling at them to slow down.

Whenever the boys spotted one of the cool teenagers, they hoped the teen would think that Trina belonged to someone else.

Samuel's heart leaped as he entered the park and saw that the girl was already there with her elegant Doberman. Just as the week before, her dog frolicked on the lawn, yet never strayed far from his attractive companion. "This time I'm going to make my move," Samuel said to himself as he released Ginger from her leash.

Ginger lunged forward, dashing to the pond where the small dogs played. Max's ears perked up, he let out a short yelp of alarm, and took off after Ginger—pulling Samuel behind him! Taken completely off guard, Samuel shouted at the top of his lungs, "Stop, Max, stop!"

But Max didn't stop. His leash, wrapped tightly around his master's wrist, meant that Samuel didn't stop, either.

That's how it happened that Samuel landed in the pond. Everyone in the park saw it, including the girl. She laughed. He was humiliated.

But on their first wedding anniversary, they laughed together at the memory of their first meeting, with Max, Ginger, and the elegant Doberman sprawled on the floor beside them.

> *The great pleasure of a dog is that you may*
> *make a fool of yourself with him and*
> *not only will he not scold you,*
> *but he will make a fool of himself, too.*
>
> Samuel Butler

The Homecoming

From a Dog Who Waited Faithfully

I knew from the way you hugged me and said good-bye that it wasn't going to be an ordinary day. Usually you'd give me a treat or two and a pat on the head before you'd leave, and then I'd settle down for a nice nap. A few hours later I'd take my place by the window and watch for you to pull into the driveway, and sure enough, you'd show up like clockwork.

This time, though, you gave me a long, long hug and a whole handful of treats. You told me to be a good dog. I'm sure I saw tears in your eyes and heard a crack in your voice. Then you picked up a duffel bag, gave me one last look, and you were gone.

Hoping against hope, I went through my usual routine of eating the treats you had given me, taking a nap, and waiting by the window, but you didn't come that day. Or the next. Or the one after that. Sure, I was well taken care of by the other people who live in this house, and for that I'm so very thankful! Not every dog is as lucky as I am, I know.

Sometimes I'd hear your voice, and I'd come running into the room, only to discover that the people were talking and laughing at a screen! It had your face on it, and I heard you talking (you even said my name!), but it wasn't the same. I guess it wasn't quite the same for anyone else, either, because all the people said was how much they missed you and wished you could come home. Me, too.

After what seemed like forever, a special day came. I could feel the excitement in the air. Suddenly everybody was smiling and laughing like they hadn't in a long time—ever since you left, as a matter of fact. There was a big flurry of activity around here, and then they all piled in the car and went away.

I paced the floor, wondering what was going on. Then something told me to go sit by the window. Suddenly I felt so happy that my tail started wagging even before I saw you! The car pulled into the driveway, and you were in it!

I couldn't believe my eyes! You saw me at the window, waved, and called my name. It was really, really you! Dashing into the house, you gave me the biggest hug of my life! And that old duffel bag? You tossed it up on a closet shelf, and I hope it stays there for a long, long time!

DOGS WAIT
FOR US FAITHFULLY.
CICERO

He is your friend,
your partner,
your defender, your dog.
You are his life,
his love, his leader.
He will be yours,
faithful and true,
to the last beat of his heart.
You owe it to him
to be worthy of such devotion.

Author Unknown

Puppy Love

Linda Alley

Our two dogs, Bob and Jake, needed some obedience training. We joined a class; I had Bob (a 50-pound Lab mix) and Steve had Jake (a 110-pound black Labrador Retriever). The instructor thought it was best to separate "the boys" during class, especially when it came to working in one long horizontal line-up.

We began working on various commands, starting with "Stay." Then came "Sit." A few giggles came from down the line. I saw the instructor shake his head and point at someone. When I heard "Down," there was out-and-out laughter and the instructor strode purposefully over to the line. I craned my neck to see what was going on down there.

Steve and Jake were next to a young teenage girl and her tiny little white powder puff of a puppy. For Jake, it was love at first sight. When Steve told Jake to sit, Jake sat—facing the puppy. Steve tried to correct Jake, but not before the instructor noticed his struggle.

Jake just kept looking longingly over at his new love. When commanded "down," Jake immediately lay down—and rolled over on his back, squirmed sideways, and nosed the puppy, his legs pawing happily at the air. Steve couldn't get Jake to stop flirting! That's when the instructor stepped in. Needless to say, Jake was moved so he could focus on being obedient.

Love would have to wait until after class!

You meet your friend, your face brightens—
you have struck gold.
Kassia

Patsy Ann

A Story of Warmth and Welcome

If you've ever sailed into the harbor of Juneau, Alaska, you've met Pasty Ann—her memorial sculpture, that is. Named the town's official greeter in 1934, she was a Bull Terrier that had been brought to Juneau as a pup.

Though deaf from birth, Patsy Ann could sense when a ship was nearing the wharf, even before it appeared on the horizon. She'd quickly trot down to the docks and await the vessel's arrival, greeting old friends and visitors alike with tail-waggin' excitement and enthusiasm. It's said that once when a ship was coming into port and people started gathering on the wrong pier, Patsy Ann looked at the crowd and then promptly trotted over another pier—which turned out to be the right one.

Most days, she made her home in hotel lobbies and local businesses, much to the delight of guests and townspeople alike. Soon post cards with her picture and other Patsy Ann mementoes were selling in gift shops around town, and she became a must-see, must-pet for any Juneau-bound traveler. Not a few rewarded her with tasty treats for her attention!

Even though rheumatism slowed her down considerably in her later years, she still made it to the docks to meet ships that pulled in and welcome its passengers as they filed down the gangplank. Today her bronze statue stands right where you would have seen her so many years ago, looking out to the harbor, waiting to welcome you home.

Kindness is the language
which the deaf can hear
and the blind can see.

Mark Twain

The Best Grilled Hamburgers I Ever Made

Laurie Harper

It was a busy, hot Saturday evening. I was grilling hamburgers while my husband, Steve, washed the car. Neither of us noticed that our four-year-old son, Mark, had made his way into the garage, accompanied by his faithful black Lab, Joe, and yellow Lab, Mikey. Barefoot, Mark somehow stepped in some broken glass. Steve said he heard the dogs barking frantically, so ran into the garage only to find Mark sitting on the floor in tears. Just as I put a plate of freshly grilled hamburgers on the counter, Steve ran into the house carrying a sobbing Mark with the Labs close behind.

The Labs each took a position by Mark's side and licked away his tears as we worked to get the glass removed from Mark's feet. Mark was laughing and crying at the same time with Joe and Mikey being so affectionate and attentive.

After we got all the glass removed, I let Steve finish the first aid and left to check on our dinner. That's when I noticed the wonderful aroma of those grilled hamburgers…and no dogs in sight.

I ran to the kitchen just in time to catch Joe and Mickey each with a hamburger in their mouths and a few grease spots on the floor! They stopped mid-chew and looked up at me with guilt written all over their faces. But how could I scold them? I smiled and said, "Bon appétit, guys!" and left them to their burgers.

We ate salad that night.

One pardons in the degree that one loves.
François de La Rochefoucauld

Learning to Trust Again

Mary Shields

Puffy came to my husband and me as a trembling little puppy in desperate need of a good situation. A toy poodle, she was as sweet as can be, but she had been roughly treated and frequently swatted with a newspaper, as we later learned. In all the years we had her, she never lost her fear of newspapers. We promised her that those days were over, and she would have a home with us as long as she lived.

She had a nose for food, as we soon discovered. Every morning we'd let her out to do her business, and one day, when I opened the door to let her back in, she had a very large doughnut in her mouth. She seemed so very pleased with herself.

I looked up and down the street but saw no one who might have given it to her. I didn't let her eat it, and thinking she might have meant it as a treat for me, I politely declined the offer. The next week, the week of Harvest, she appeared at the door again clutching a doughnut, this time one with orange frosting and sprinkles on top. Again, no one was around.

Then one morning the following week she didn't come to the door at her usual time, so I stepped out to look for her. Walking up to our back fence, I spied her over in the next yard, where our neighbors were having breakfast on their patio. I was right in time to see them reach down and hand her a big doughnut! Mystery solved.

Though Puffy had known the unkindness of people, she allowed herself to trust again, learning the difference between a hand with a rolled-up newspaper and the hand holding out a doughnut. She reminded me how important it is to never give up on love.

The remedy of all blunders,
the cure of blindness, the cure of crime, is love.
Ralph Waldo Emerson

Barkley's Big Splash

Sue Englert

When my husband and I adopted our first Labrador Retriever, we envisioned him getting old with us. Yet we knew it wouldn't happen, considering how young we were at the time and that Labs, like other large breeds, don't live terribly long lives. Our beloved first Lab, Brando, was with us for ten wonderful years.

When our second Lab, Barkley, joined the family, we were thrilled when he was still healthy and active after ten years. Then he reached eleven, and twelve, and even thirteen! But then he suddenly started to act like an old dog.

My husband and I, along with our two teen-agers, knew that time was taking its toll. We were feeling lumps under his fur, and our vet told us that he had tumors. Because of severe arthritis, his back legs wouldn't bend, so he couldn't go up or down stairs, he couldn't run, and he definitely couldn't jump up on the bed any more. He also had cataracts, so his vision wasn't what it had once been.

We were afraid to leave him at home for long periods of time, so we took him on trips with us, sneaking him into hotels that allowed small dogs—Barkley weighed around 90 pounds. We knew he was in pain, but he was still smiling and wiggling and wagging, so we tried our best to keep him going.

Barkley loved the beach—all the swimming, and playing, and especially lying in the warm, soft sand. When we all knew that Barkley's days were numbered, we planned a short family trip to the beach to give him one last romp in the sand and the surf. We fixed a soft palette in the van for him to ride the three hours to Hilton Head.

Our reservations were at a hotel on the beach that allowed small dogs, but when we got there, we discovered that our room was on the fourth floor. This was a problem. Barkley couldn't go up the stairs, and no dogs were allowed in the elevator, much less 90-pound dogs that weren't even supposed to be in the hotel.

By some miracle, however, we were able to switch to a room on the ground floor without being identified as dog-sneaking frauds—perfect! Right out the sliding door to a patio, and just a short walk across the pool deck to the beach.

My husband put Barkley on his leash, and we all headed out for a quick walk in the sand just as it was starting to get dark. He seemed so happy to be there—there was even somewhat of a spring in his step! One of the great things about him was that we didn't even have to hold the leash when we walked him—he would just drag it along as he heeled right beside whichever human was walking with him. He would practically walk himself and never run off.

After a short time on the beach, it was getting later and getting darker, so we decided to head back to the room. As usual, Barkley was walking himself. Suddenly, as we entered the pool deck, he veered sharply off to the right. It happened so fast that we couldn't quite grab the leash, and before we could stop him, he plunged right into the pool! Needless to say, he made quite a splash!

My husband immediately dived in after him, because Barkley could no longer swim with arthritic legs. Swimmers were startled, onlookers were laughing, and our "small" dog's cover was completely blown!

We think that Barkley might have seen the pretty blue lights shining in the water, and through his cataracts he thought it would be a great place to lie down. After my husband pulled him out, the dog seemed unfazed. He acted like it was perfectly natural and completely intentional to take an impromptu dip in the hotel pool, despite the fact he could no longer swim.

> *Happy the man who early learns*
> *the wide chasm that lies between*
> *his wishes and his powers.*
> Johann von Goethe

Just Nuisance

A Story of Faithful Military Service

A Great Dane destined for great things was born in South Africa in 1937. Bought as a pup by Benjamin Chaney, he was taken to Simon's Town, a Naval Base, where he quickly made friends with Royal Navy sailors. He liked to take naps on the gangways of ships, forcing sailors to walk around the big dog, which they did good-naturedly, and they affectionately named him Nuisance.

When sailors on leave would board the train to Cape Town, Nuisance followed. Trouble is, dogs were not allowed on trains, and a Great Dane isn't an easily concealed passenger. Much to the annoyance of the sailors, conductors would evict the stowaway at the next station. That's why the sailors decided to enlist Nuisance in the Royal Navy, which would entitle him as a member of the military to a seat on the train.

When the Recruiting Officer asked the dog's name, a sailor said, "Nuisance." "Nuisance what?" the officer asked. "Just Nuisance, sir."

The Great Dane became Ordinary Seaman Just Nuisance in the Royal Navy, eligible for a seat on the train. Hassles from conductors ceased. Not only did he get to ride the rails, Just Nuisance obviously performed his duties admirably, because he was later promoted to Able Seaman.

During World War II, Just Nuisance proved a morale booster for military troops serving at the South Atlantic Station. He also appeared at promotional events, raising money for the war effort. Upon his death in 1944, Just Nuisance was put to rest with full military honors.

Homeward Bound

Laurie Harper

Sammie, a Maltese, and Charlotte, a black Lab, decided one cold wintery day that they would go exploring. We figure that as everyone was hustling out the door for school and work that morning, the last person out of the house would slam the door shut.

A blustery wind was all it took for the door to pop open and Sammie and Charlotte to pop out. Unfortunately, our pampered Maltese was unaware of her size or breed. She probably thought she was just as tough and big as her pal, Charlotte.

Our teenaged son was the first one home that afternoon, and as he drove up to the house and saw the open door, he gasped. He knew full well how adventuresome the dogs were. Sure enough, no dogs were in the house. He bundled up for the weather and started walking the neighborhood, calling their names. No answer. Mark phoned me at work telling me about the situation, and I couldn't get home fast enough.

As I pulled into the driveway, I could see big Charlotte by Mark's side, but no sign of little Sammie. By this time snow was coming down fast and furiously. Mark told me that he had found Charlotte at the top of the hill at the end of the street, so we started trudging up the icy hill, theorizing that they had travelled together.

Just as the tears started swelling in our eyes at the thought of a lost and confused Maltese buried in a blizzard, we spied a little speck of white wiggling towards us from the top of the hill. Her little legs, each one sinking in snow almost deeper than she was tall, made her progress slow—and comical! Our tears turned to shrieks of laughter as we clambered up the hill to retrieve her, as we ourselves were slipping and sliding through the swirling snow.

Once in the house, both dogs looked quite pleased with the way the day had gone. They wolfed down their dinner, lapped from their water bowl, and then settled down in front of the fireplace for a nice evening's snooze. We couldn't get over the image of a big black Lab and a tiny white Maltese frolicking in a blizzard together, but just like the movie, they were always homeward bound.

A man travels the world over in search of what he needs and returns home to find it.

George Moore

WHEN YOU GO TO BED AT NIGHT,

HAVE FOR YOUR PILLOW THREE THINGS—

LOVE, HOPE, AND FORGIVENESS.

AND YOU WILL AWAKEN IN THE MORNING

WITH A SONG IN YOUR HEART.

VICTOR HUGO

The Life of Murphy

Patricia Mitchell

Before church begins on Sunday mornings, I get to catch up on Murphy and Mew Mew's latest goings-on. Murphy is a Rat Terrier belonging to Bob and Melvadean, and Mew Mew the army cat lives with them while Mew Mew's mom serves in the military.

"Murphy and Mew Mew are pretty good buddies," says Bob, "but once in a while Murphy reverts to doing what any self-respecting dog would do. She chases Mew Mew all over the house until Melvadean has had enough of the ruckus." When Melvadean shouts "No!" the animals stop in their tracks and generally head for the water dish to have a relaxing drink together.

Even more than Mew Mew, Murphy responds to any rustle or rattle that might in any way have to do with food. She can be sound asleep—her preferred position being flopped on her back with four legs sticking straight up in the air—until she hears one of them heading toward the kitchen. Suddenly she's fully alert and flipping and wiggling frantically trying to right herself so she can run to the refrigerator! Now how long has it been since her last meal? An hour, maybe?

She's a good dog, but of course she has her share of habits that aren't about to be broken. When either Bob or Melvadean is talking on the kitchen phone, for instance, she dances around, wags her tail like crazy, and starts barking to the point that they're forced to give her a treat just to get her to quit.

They guess that someone in her past would give her treats to hush her up, and she figures, "Hey, if it worked then, it will work now." So, as you can imagine, plenty of treats are kept right by the telephone.

Despite her healthy bark, the couple doesn't look to Murphy for burglar protection. That's because she figures that anyone who comes to the door has come to see her. The mail carrier, package deliverer, service providers–they're all her best friends forever. Of course, what she would do if one of her BFFs were to climb through the window, they fortunately have not had the opportunity to find out. But if the intruder came armed with treats, it's not hard to guess that he'd get a warm, friendly, tail-waggin' reception.

But that's the way it is with most of our canine friends, isn't it? They don't ask many questions or judge the way we look before they'll give us the time of day, but offer us their love just the way we are. And I guess that's why we're happy to return the favor. Those of us who love dogs know there's no other choice but to take them as they are, habits and quirks and things only a dog could tell you why.

Next Sunday I'm going to hear more what's it's like to "love one another"–even when the "other" turns out to be a cat.

THERE IS NOTHING ON THIS EARTH
MORE TO BE PRIZED
THAN TRUE FRIENDSHIP.
THOMAS AQUINAS

Saying Goodbye

Laurie Harper

Like dog owners and pet lovers everywhere, I have had my share of grief, as I've said good-bye to many beloved pets at the end of their lives. I know I shouldn't compare the death of a pet to that of a relative or friend, but when a pet is like a member of the family, I think the heartache is much the same.

It seems like only yesterday that our little Maltese puppy came into our lives. That little white ball of fur melted our hearts the moment we saw her. We named her Lucy. We had never had a little dog before, so we were surprised to see her keep up with our two big Labradors, chasing squirrels and rabbits in the backyard, perching on the living room sofa looking out the window, and guarding the house just like them.

Twelve short years later I was holding our little Lucy in my arms at the vet's office while my husband and I waited for her doctor to return with his verdict. I cuddled her, kissed her sweet head, and told her how much I loved her over and over again.

When the doctor came in the room, he didn't need to say a word. I could see the answer in his eyes. He said we could take as much time as we needed to say our goodbyes.

My heart aches now as I remember him trying to comfort us by assuring us that we did everything medically possible for Lucy, but it was time for us to do the most compassionate thing. She had contracted hepatitis and was now a very sick dog.

My husband took her from my arms and held her like he always did over his shoulder. It was as if she knew. We huddled around her, lifting up our prayers, and she had a peaceful end to a full life. As sad as it was, we knew we had done the right thing. Suddenly it felt like a heavy weight was lifted off of us. The tough decision was made, and we knew she was no longer in pain.

It is still hard to reminisce about our very unique little dog that brought so much life and joy into our home. We hold our memories of her close to our hearts. Even though we know that other dogs will join our family and they will surely bring us the same kind of fond memories, there will never be another Lucy.

What the heart has once owned and had,
it shall never lose.

Henry Ward Beecher

A Convertible, a Corgi, and a Squirrel

Laurie Harper

What happens when you put a corgi in a red convertible, drive with the top down, and the corgi sees a squirrel? This is what happens: said corgi, Guinness, forgets he can't fly. He leaps out of the car with all four paws extended.

Panicked, we pulled over immediately. Looking back in the direction Guinness flew, we watched as that log-like body stopped, dropped and rolled and rolled and rolled! He got up, slightly dazed, and glanced around, perhaps hoping there were no witnesses to his failed airborne adventure. He slowly made his way back to the car with his big ears down and a grin on his face that seemed to say, "Oh, I didn't mean to do that. It's the squirrel's fault."

Yeah, right. Hop back in, buster. And next time, don't just look, but think before you leap!

Self-control is the quality
that distinguishes the fittest to survive.
George Bernard Shaw

EXUBERANCE IS BEAUTY.

WILLIAM BLAKE

See Me! See Me!

From Someone Who Has Love To Give

Hey there! Yes, I mean you! I saw you walk past my kennel, and I can't believe you didn't stop to say hello! Well, maybe you need to check out my yappy neighbor over there, or the handsome fellow who seems to get all the attention.

Or maybe you're looking around at all the noses pressed against kennels, and you're feeling kinda sad. You wish you could adopt every single one of us, don't you? I wish you could, too. I wish you could give all the dogs in the whole world a loving home, good food, and a comfy place to sleep at night. Sigh! No one person can do that, though. But you know what? You can save one of us (me? me? me?). That's something one person can do!

Ooooh, look, look! You're headed in my direction! See me? You do, you do! Now you're saying something to that nice lady who gives me food, cleans my kennel, and takes me for walks in the yard. She's getting my leash! Oh, no, is she taking me outside right when we're getting to know each other? I want to stay here with you!

Clunk! goes the wire latch and click! goes the leash on my collar. She's handing the leash to you! Yippee! We're going outside together! What could be better? I'm going to do everything I can to win your heart, because you've already won mine a million times over!

THERE IS NO DUTY
WE SO MUCH UNDERRATE
AS THE DUTY OF
BEING HAPPY.
ROBERT LOUIS STEVENSON

Neighborhood Dogs

Patricia Mitchell

"They have a bark-a-thon every morning,"
I heard a co-worker say. "Mine gets out on the
deck and barks, and the dog living two houses
down does the same thing."

Being the keeper of cats, I was taken aback
by the bark-a-thon business. More specifically,
I wondered about the peace of my co-worker's
neighborhood and contemplated the plight of
the hapless residents who lived between those
two dog-inhabited decks.

Fortunately, in my area there are no daily
bark-a-thons. In fact the dogs who live here,
like the people, are all part of the ambience of
the neighborhood. And like each one of us, each
dog has a unique story to tell.

There's Maggie, a small wiry dog who was
found wandering, lost and hungry, a block or
two away. She was taken in and given a home
by a kindly neighbor who had recently lost her
beloved dog, another stray of many years ago.

Once when I was chatting with Maggie's new mom, I offered to take the dog's leash for a spell. Her diminutive size belies her formidable strength! Walking with Maggie is like trying to stop a runaway train. After a few minutes, my arm feeling several inches longer than before, I handed the leash back to my neighbor.

Then there's Diesel and Leila, both big shelter dogs with even bigger issues. Yet months of constant love, guidance, and training by their adoptive families has brought out the best in both dogs. Diesel, an active, energetic dog, runs laps up and down the divided street without straying into yards or cornering walkers anymore. Leila walks calmly at the end of a leash with no sign of fear or anxiety.

Some dogs I know by sight only…the big, long-haired golden dog that looks like a lion at first glance…the tiny fluffy pup walked by a large balding man…the spunky Dalmatian whose family brought home an adopted baby…

and in my mind's eye, the beloved brindle dog who used to trot alongside the longtime neighbor who now walks alone.

From time to time I think about getting a dog. But then I'd have to face the family cats, and their yowls of protest could rival any bark-a-thon anywhere. So I'd better think again.

In each action we must look beyond the
action at our past, present, and future state,
and at others whom it affects,
and see the relations of all those things.
And then we shall be very cautious.

Blaise Pascal

Gotcha!

Phyllis Camp

Could we depend on our Westie, Cotton, to guard our home from burglars? No. Coyotes? No. But when it comes to squirrels and cats, we're safe!

We have two dog doors, one door that goes out onto our screened-in porch, and then another from the porch leading to our backyard. Whenever Cotton spies a cat or squirrel in our yard, she gets really quiet. She approaches the porch as if on tiptoe and eases through the dog door one leg at a time.

The door doesn't make a noise or swing back and forth, because she lets the flap glide silently over her back. Then she slinks over to the door that opens to the backyard, going so slowly that she actually starts trembling in anticipation. It's hysterical to watch her moving in slow motion as she tries to sneak up on the trespassing critters!

At exactly the right moment, she bursts through the outside door, and without so much as a squeak, she lunges at the startled cat, who dives under the fence, and she sends all the hapless squirrels scampering up the nearest tree. Now the game is on!

She rushes back to the house, dashes through the dog doors (this time sending the flaps flying!) and scampers up on the back of the couch to look out the front window just in case the cat or squirrels think they're safe.

Once satisfied that the coast is clear, she races to the backyard for a final check on the where-abouts of those pesky critters. In all her zeal to clear our property of critters, however, she frequently misjudges the dog door and smacks headlong into our sliding glass door. Ouch! Believe me, that calms our guard dog down for a little while! But thanks to Cotton, we're safe from attack by cats and squirrels—at least for the next 10 minutes.

Be always resolute with the present hour.
Every moment is of infinite value.

Johann von Goethe

Mr. Guinness' Good Influence

Laurie Harper

Two years ago Mr. Guinness entered the picture. Though Megan was carrying a full load at school, working a part-time job, and was barely able to afford rent and gas for her car, she adopted a puppy. "He's free, Mom!" she excitedly announced. Okay, there is no such thing as a free dog, but being the dog lover that I am, and after seeing a picture of him, I understood why she couldn't resist. He's part corgi, part Australian shepherd, and part a little bit of everything else. He came with the name Guinness.

The following semester was busier than ever for Megan, so now Guinness is living temporarily with Grandpa and Grandma until she finishes school. Though we love our Grand-dog to pieces, we've had to make serious changes to our lifestyle. No, I'm not talking about doggy-proofing our home—I mean changing the way we live.

We can no longer watch TV because Guinness likes to watch TV all too much. If a dog appears on the screen, he barks at it and tries to crawl inside the TV. He growls incessantly at things he doesn't like, and the list of growl-worthy people, animals, scenes, shows, and products increases with every viewing hour.

So now my husband and I read a lot more. And since Guinness insists on a walk every day, we exercise a lot more, too. Nap in the afternoon? Good idea, Guinness. We all need a little time out.

I guess having Guinness come to our house has been a very good thing. When it's time for him to go back with Megan, it will be up to us to keep up our healthy habits!

Smoky

A Story of Comfort and Care

One day during the Second World War on the South Pacific island of New Guinea, a lost and confused Yorkie puppy wandered across the battlefield. Corporal William Wynne found her, took her back to his barracks, and named her Smoky. Her high energy and aptitude for acrobatics entertained the troops, while her comforting presence soothed jangled nerves and lifted battle-weary hearts. Smoky offered a welcome touch of home in a faraway place.

A time when Wynne landed in the hospital, his buddies brought in Smoky for a visit. Not only did the lively Yorkie cheer her rescuer, but she brought a smile to wan faces throughout the ward. Soon she was a regular at the hospital, and for the next dozen years, provided unconditional acceptance, love, and comfort to patients.

In the 1950s, medical professionals in America and elsewhere began to train dogs to work with patients not only in hospitals, but in nursing homes, mental wards, and long-term care facilities.

Therapy dogs have brought comfort and relief to untold numbers of people suffering the effects of trauma or recovering from disasters of all kinds. The dogs are helpful in reaching emotionally scarred adults and children, and they are often brought in to assist counselors and mental health professionals.

Golden Retrievers, with their gentle temperament and people-friendly ways, were among the first formally trained therapy dogs to roam the corridors of medical institutions. Over the years, however, many other breeds have joined their ranks. What they all have in common is a calm, friendly temperament and amenable to petting, stroking, hugging, and cuddling. And now, even though they don't meet all the doggie qualifications, there are therapy cats, rabbits, fish, and birds to help bring out the smiles!

GOODNESS IS THE ONLY
INVESTMENT THAT
NEVER FAILS.
HENRY DAVID THOREAU

The Hunter

Patricia Mitchell

A longtime hunter, Tom prized his hunting dog, a German Wirehaired Pointer named Sticks. True to his breed, Sticks bonded closely with Tom, his wife, and their two young sons.

Sticks was an energetic pup, banned from the house by Tom's wife—which was fine with him, because he thrived being outdoors. A smart dog, Sticks learned commands quickly and how to retrieve with ease. He was always eager to play, run in the park, and go for early-morning walks. Craving outdoor adventure, his favorite time of year was the same as Tom's—hunting season!

A slight chill to the wind and a quiet rustle in the house in the predawn hours was all it took to signal that the great day had arrived at last. As Tom would load the truck, Sticks could hardly contain himself, yipping and yelping with excitement. "Come on, Sticks!" was something Tom only had to say once, because before the words were out of his mouth, Sticks was in the truck and rarin' to go.

As teens, the boys joined Tom and Sticks on their hunting expeditions. The memories they made together meant more than anyone's hunting prowess, although Sticks held onto his competitive edge, no matter how frosty the ground or damp the duck blind.

Then everything changed.

A cough that lasted too long and frequent shortness of breath brought Tom to his physician's office. After multiple tests, the doctors discovered lung disease with no known cause. The condition was exacerbated by exposure to grass, mold, pollen, and other elements, so there were no more hunting trips for Tom.

Or for Sticks.

Tom's condition worsened, and less than six months after his diagnosis, Tom needed to use oxygen. Since even going outside to Sticks' kennel was a strain, the faithful hunting companion was allowed inside the house. Fearing the worst from her husband's high-energy hound, Tom's wife put breakables away and moved small tables and valued lamps to another, closed-off room.

But she needn't have worried. Sticks proved every inch the perfect houseguest. He walked through the kitchen and into the living room where Tom lay on the couch with his breathing apparatus. Gently and carefully, the dog settled himself next to the couch with his paw resting lightly on the air tube, seemingly knowing that this was his master's lifeline.

He seemed to know, too, that he'd never again hear the early morning rustle, the truck pulling out of the garage before dawn, or the chirps of wildlife waking as the sun rose over a glassy lake. And he was okay with that. He had what was most important—family and the gift of life and breath.

Seek not that the things which happen
should happen as you wish;
but wish the things which happen
to be as they are, and you will have
a tranquil flow of life.

Epictetus

Barry
A Story of Commitment and Courage

For over 300 years, St. Bernard dogs have been famous for rescuing snow-stranded travelers. Their sense of direction, ability to locate people buried in an avalanche, and resistance to bitter cold equip them to handle their risky and dangerous work.

One of the most notable St. Bernard rescue dogs was Barry. Born in 1800, he lived at a monastery located in the St. Bernard Pass, a treacherous Alpine route between Italy and Switzerland. There, the monks housed and trained a team of dogs to help them in their rescue efforts after severe snowstorms.

Barry, credited with saving over 40 lives, is best known for his daring rescue of an injured boy trapped on a narrow, icy ledge. Covered in snow, the boy faced certain death as the storm grew fiercer and blizzard conditions prevented the monks from climbing up to him. But the storm didn't deter Barry.

Slowly the dog pulled himself up to the ledge where the boy, now fallen asleep in the snow, was stranded. By licking his face, Barry woke him, but the storm still raged and no monk was able to reach the ledge to offer further help. That's when the boy wrapped his arms around Barry, enabling the dog to draw him off the ledge and pull him to safety.

Barry's brave and honorable service to stranded travelers, pilgrims, and soldiers ended when he died of old age. Today Barry's preserved body is on display at the Natural History Museum in Berne, Switzerland.

Adversity has the effect of eliciting talents which in prosperous times would have lain dormant.

Horace

Our Baby

Phyllis Camp

Cotton is the second West Highland White Terrier my husband and I have had for a pet. Though all Westies look alike, their personalities are very different. While our first Westie, Kessie, was an independent-minded dog, Cotton is just the opposite. She's an especially people-oriented dog, and she really likes to snuggle.

She has two stuffed animals, Baby Lamb and Baby Squirrel, that she sleeps with, and she has a silly little ritual she goes through every night with the Babies. When we're doing the dishes after dinner, she goes into the bedroom and brings one or both of the Babies out to us, whining the whole time. Now she is two years old, and you would think she would outgrow this! But I'm very glad she hasn't. She treats the Babies as if they're living creatures.

When we finish the dishes, we sit down to watch TV. That's when Cotton brings the Babies to "Daddy" by going back around his chair and on his right side so Daddy will reach down and pet her and the Babies. Cotton eventually lies across Daddy's feet, encouraging him to pet her by pushing her nose on him until he does what she wants. The next thing you know she's up in the chair with you and you don't know how she did it! We wouldn't give up this Baby for anything!

A friend is a gift
you give yourself.
Robert Louis Stevenson

The Girlfriend

JoLynne Walz Martinez

"We don't need any more animals around here," my husband used to tell me. Yes, I was the one who kept bringing them home. We had a dog, two cats, and tank full of fish…and then there was that pet hedgehog I kept oohing and aaahing over at the pet store.

When our daughter was born, though, I had my hands full, and I finally had to agree. I didn't need another animal to take care of or mouth to feed.

How had my parents managed it all, I wondered, with three little girls and an endless parade of pets? There had been dogs, cats, gerbils, goldfish, parakeets…and whatever else one of us girls would bring home.

So I was surprised when my husband came back from walking our dog, Al, one night and called out to me. "Sweetie, come here." Sitting there in the hallway was a brindled dog with matted fur limping on a sore paw.

"It was hurt and rummaging through a trash can for food," my husband said apologetically. "When it started following us home, I didn't have the heart to turn it away."

"It" turned out to be a girl, and she did have a sweet face. Still, I knew she couldn't stay with us. We already had Al—Big Al—a 100-pound black Labrador Retriever and pointer mix that we had raised from a pup. Interestingly, though, for a big guy who was usually quite territorial, he didn't seem at all bothered to be sharing the house with…not knowing what her name was, we started calling her "girlfriend."

"Okay," I sighed. "She can stay here until we find out who she belongs to." Of course, we started by checking her collar. She was wearing one, but there was no tag. No microchip. No one was looking for a dog of her description.

While we were looking, I learned that she cowered in fear whenever I picked up a broom or a mop or anything that looked like a stick, so she must have suffered abuse. We also learned, much to our dismay, that she was not house-broken. And she wouldn't stop trying to tree our cats.

No, she couldn't stay with us.

We started looking for a new home for the sweet brindled girl who really wanted to be loved, but needed much more training and attention than we could give at that time in our lives.

There was a family that took her home on trial, but it didn't work out, and so the girlfriend was right back with us. The cats returned to hiding. Our Al, though, accepted the girlfriend as if she had never been gone.

I really didn't have the time, but figured I'd better get serious with housebreaking and Girlfriend (by this time, the dog thought that was her name) was a quick learner. She even learned that the kitties are our friends.

Still, no one thought of her as a permanent member of our household. We considered ourselves a foster family, sure that eventually we could find Girlfriend her forever home.

And then Al got sick. Really sick. As happens so often with big dogs, his heart was failing, and he went downhill fast. Eventually, we realized he was suffering too much, and that it was time to release him from his pain. The veterinarian came to our house.

It was pouring rain when the vet arrived, shaking off the damp as he stepped into our home.

Our daughter was very brave and chose to stay with us. As we were patting Al dog and telling him how much he was loved, the vet held a stethoscope to Al's chest, listening intently.

Eventually, that big guy's heart stopped.

And at that very moment, a tremendous clap of thunder shook the house.

"He's gone," the vet said in a quiet voice.

We were all crying, and my daughter's eyes were big in her face.

"Mommy, does it always thunder like that when someone dies?"

While the vet tended to Al dog's body, my husband stepped in to explain that, no, it doesn't always.

Then I realized there was still a dog in the room. Girlfriend had been sitting there all along, quiet and unnoticed. "Somehow Big Al knew," I thought. "He was the only one who accepted her. He brought her home."

"Come here, Girlfriend," I said, giving her a big hug and kissing her head.

We had just lost a beloved companion with such a big heart that it had gone out in a clap of thunder. And we had gained a new little brindled Girlfriend who turned out to be a champion Frisbee catcher, who sleeps next to our bed, and who I find every morning waiting expectantly for us to wake and begin a new day with her.

Of course, she will never replace Big Al in our hearts. And we definitely did not need another animal in our house. But it turned out that—even though we didn't know it—we did need Girlfriend.

Change indeed is painful,
yet ever needful.

Thomas Carlyle

Sandy's Room

Laurie Harper

We were visiting my grandparents in a neigh-
boring town when I discovered the puppy that
would become our one and only beloved family
dog.

My grandparent's neighbor's dog had a litter
of puppies that were six weeks old. I was young
myself, only four at the time. As I was playing
outside, I caught sight of those frolicking, oh-so-
adorable puppies next door. The neighbor told
me I could certainly have one, if my parents said
it was okay—and they did! I was ecstatic!

When it was time to leave Grandma and
Grandpa's house, I scooped up my new friend in
my arms, slid in the backseat of the car, and let
her snuggle up on my lap the whole way. From
then on, we were inseparable. I loved him from
the start, and in no time my whole family did,
too.

My Dad had grown up on a farm and never
had a dog reside in the house. So, he told my
sister and me that if we were going to have a

dog, there were rules, one of which was that the dog was not allowed in our bedroom.

My sister and I implemented Plan B. We went to the local grocery store and picked out the best large box we could find so we could make a suitable bed for Sandy. You would have thought we were at a furniture store shopping for a real bed the way we fussed over just the right size box!

When we finally made a choice and brought it home, we lined the bottom with an old blanket and a make-shift pillow. To make sure it was comfortable, we crawled in and tried it out ourselves. (After all, Dad didn't say anything about us not being allowed in the dog's bedroom!) We pronounced the space quite cozy. At night, we gated off the kitchen and that became Sandy's master suite.

Sandy had many sweet nicknames, but Dad called her Fleabag. Sandy didn't care, though, because she answered to it as enthusiastically as she would any of our more complimentary monikers.

Though Dad acted as if he didn't have much feeling for her, it wasn't true. One night when Sandy didn't come home, Dad was searching the neighborhood right along with the rest of us, worried and anxious, until she was found.

As an imaginative preschooler, I was quite content to create my own fun. Our laid-back cat was my willing baby doll that I dressed in my old baby outfits, and Sandy was an honored guest at my tea parties. Like our cat, Sandy would let me fit her with bonnets and necklaces without even a whine or a whimper. I'm sure the reward of a cookie or two helped ease any canine embarrassment.

Sandy played hide-n-seek with me and my friends, guarded our make-shift tent for our summer campouts, and licked my scrapes as I learned to ride a bike. She was my nurse when I was sick, and even got to lie on the sofa with me without Dad getting mad at her.

As I grew older and spent more time with school activities and a part-time job, Sandy welcomed the chance to take longer naps and spend the day with my mom as she worked around the house. Even Dad didn't seem to mind having Sandy sleep at his feet as he read the evening paper.

Many years later, when I married, we decided that Sandy, being a very senior dog, would be happier staying in the only home she had ever known. Dad informed me that Sandy was going to get my old bedroom. I smiled and told him I thought that was a great idea.

Until one has loved an animal,
a part of one's soul remains unawakened.

Anatole France

WHAT A BLESSING IT IS
TO HAVE A BEST FRIEND
WHO TOUCHES YOUR LIFE
AND LEAVES A PAWPRINT
ON YOUR HEART FOREVER.

'